Till We Have Faces

Poems, 1966-2015

By Robert Loomis

Introduction

With a heartfelt thanks to all the poets who've preceded me, I offer this selection of poems written from 1966 to 2015. These have been reworked many times. They represent a small part of my total poetic output over these past five decades. I hope the reader enjoys them.

© Robert Loomis, 2018

Are You Ready?
(In Memory of Bob Kaufman)

Are you ready for laminated Jesus eyes
squeezing through four-way intersections
before the light turns red?

For Okie caviar oozing gently through the cracks of
dawn?

For urgent Siamese washing machines
cha-cha-cha-ing through ballrooms of U-joints?

For earthmovers reeking of primordial slime
and sinking into pallorous moonbeams?

Then put on your polkadot tunafish aura
your New Age sofabed sombrero
and walk don't run
to the nearest creamy peanutbutter exit

jiving out into the distantly relative universe
to watch musical angels glide through eponymous
ecliptics
into a leafy den redolent of the platinum plutonium
virus!

As The Song Goes

I look at the few photos of my Mother's older sister Jessie who died at age 7 of diphtheria, departed early for a flight to heaven.

I think of the loss these many decades gone and all who felt that loss now also gone.

The lacy dress my Mother wore in one photo with Jessie is still neatly folded in a plastic bag in my box of family mementos, yellow now, not white, but aging better than the little girl who wore it, better than any of us who came after.

That whole time and place now utterly gone and all the people in it circa 1910 or 1915 and yet some descendants remain as proof it did once exist and lead to this for us, to our lives also so soon to pass.

Ascension Music Memo

Reach for words, for radios, for music to relay some melody, any melody no matter what: garbanzas, alphabet soup, corazon … something from the realm of freedom. Music of the spheres to bathe the ears. A joyous noise, mirth on earth even for just a short while. And go on rising, whirling upward away from inertia, up to the next story in the mind's tendentious tenements. Reeking of rocknroll, seeking shadows of past & future events, wondering how time passes so quickly. Flick joy off the end of your herbal cigaret soul. Let the ashes drop onto your coffee-table heart and into the lap of hope to teach the sharp knowledge of who gets burned to fuel this grand & clumsy ascension.

Be Ready

You stand tall though half-starved
teeth chattering,
left out in the cold again,
cheeks wet with rain or tears,
who knows, who cares?
You no longer worry over such trifles.
The point is not to seek relief,
that comes soon enough;
the point's to be alert
in case your ship comes in
or even passes close enough
for you to wave goodbye.

Bound for Glory

Even now glory is approaching at top speed, ETA just when we least expect it ... a large, revolving headlight suddenly rushing right at us, larger and larger and then WHAM! pushing us down the tracks till we drop off the cowcatcher into the dirt and rocks along life's roadbed ... journey's end for another solar-powered water tank.

HONK! HONK! The geese of the season herald the crossing, the shunting of the car to the sidetrack, the end of the line, that's all she wrote ... meet me at the station and we'll rail against fate, sing the railroad blues, throw another log on the fire, get all steamed up over nothing, flash through town so fast it'll be as though it never happened ... but the rush feels so fine!

Chrysanthemum Kiss
(For Salvador Dali)

Your mind's eye's brush paints a loving revolution amid pagan rites and the promise of a rich life.

Your mouth is on mine and the road disappears stolen by the distance. The pianist's hands are chrysanthemums glistening dew.

Your eyes fly away & butterflies flutter over keyboard beaches playing lighthouse notes to guide us into a tawny port lit with sunrise colors!

Clutter,
mostly clutter
all these words;
noise,
mostly noise
all these songs,
intended
to capture
some of life's
transcendent
beauty, some
of life's horrific
clutter
of cruelty
to one another
to
Mother Earth
and Father Sky.
And
yes, love,
acts of love.
Sing
in beauty,
sing in beauty.
Walk
in beauty,
walk in beauty
even
amid the
clutter.

Djuna

She would awake to animals and the brown page waiting like a trench to be dug. She would be indisposed then until noon talking with visiting writers and petting her hornets.

She expected nothing to change and played blues harp from noon till 1, then took the sun when it was there for the taking.

In prolific years she wrote lanterns and searchlights in a dark book, stringing herself out endlessly on the sky, a gay kite exposed to the clouds until early evening when she would dine on aesthetic problems and broomsticks ("a rather pedantic witch," she once jested while digesting her thoughts).

Finally then to the drawing room with a magazine to clip photos for an album of superfluous visions depicting an elegant grotto wherein she hid her innermost self, a tendril in a clay jar whose mouth whistled or moaned according to which way the wind was blowing.

Gallery House at Big Sur

The coastline beckons seductively to the few puffy clouds while awaiting the return of those who lived here before.

Truly "a wild coast and lonely," even with the thousands of vehicles and tourists.

The ocean doesn't care, just keeps on rollin' & tumblin' with that ancient geological timing whispering and roaring "we're comin' t' git ya!" to the rocks.

Trees just look on and a few restored condors grace the sky, all dwarfed by this rugged stretch of sheer beauty.

We stand at the edge, breathing deeply to fill our lungs and hearts with magic.

Ghost Writer In The Literary Sky

Climb aboard a genre that ultimately trots up a box canyon with no formal outlet, concerning itself more with sagebrush pillows where we'll rest our bow-legged minds after a hard day's ride rounding up words.

The chuck wagon serves a free-association sausage with meters chopped finely into verbal chili con carne and a solipsistic salsa.

Yes, ma'am, we are caballeros riding the open plains of prose poesy. Return with us now to those early days of yesteryear ... a fiery metaphorical horse with the speed of light and a hearty "HI-YO Silvertongue!"

Thus we search the open range for prosody amid the literary gold rush. Soon we'll unsaddle our horses and turn them out to pasture. We'll sit on the old front porch, feet up on the rail, and play old songs on our cowboy-angel mouth harps to embellish another day's versifying.

In my otherwise empty saddlebags you'll find trail dust of a thousand years of galloping western verse. Vaya con palabras, amigos!

God
there is
a lot of
blather
signifying something
maybe love or
lust
or something
even finer if
such
a thing
can even exist
in
this world
of improbable rules
and
mutable tools
for lyrical living
a
sort of
linear accelerator for
symphonies
of musical
lines dreamed up
by
melodious madmen
and madwomen of
uncommon
verbal acuity
a perpetual arriving
in
the form of moving words.

Godforsaken Blues

Eyes wary as feral cats' they ride public transit to nowhere ... trying to stay warm in forever winter ... headphones connected only to voices in their heads ... listening reluctantly to truly crazy shit ... riding from one end of the line to the other, then changing trains and repeating ... texting God for a dry place to sleep without being rousted ... seeking miracle cigaret butt or swig of wine or hit of smack or crack or speed to cushion the long ride to not-so-golden dawn ... making no friends that last longer than shared medication ... lovers long gone or never ... sometimes found frozen in doorways of office buildings of mega-corps ... the same old song you've heard before, the Godforsaken Blues ... all restrictions apply ... see writing on wall for details ...

If Perhaps

If perhaps the long descent into conversational voltage of shadows and fate eyes peering through the mist can unleash the burden of pent-up laughter within us, can shake down the tresses of Mother Earth's delights

If perhaps imagination can respond to squandered kisses from lips of feminine landscapes like waterfalls over diamond doorways

If perhaps this low forehead can be pulled up the flagstaff to flap in moistened sunlight and signal the operator of the battered jukebox to play some upbeat tune then perhaps memory's faded codas can orchestrate our voices and though I am enslaved to radar and other high technologies you'll still come to see me through enchanted eyes and call my unlisted number

I'll hum digital parables of love, sing mountains of love green with the growth of a million years of osprey-nested treetops and when I hear you ring I'll answer in pieces of cut, colored glass
that you'll assemble into a kaleidoscopic window through which the sacred sun will shine like polished mirrors, will shine like wild eyes in a freshly-watered springtime meadow after a shower of raindrop stars

if perhaps

The Pair Who Found A Renaissance

There was a man who rose from behind a list of
names at the convention to become a souvenir, a
famous signature, that is
the public loved him.

He wore smiles as flowers and stirred
old ashes into the compost
to spark new flames.

It was painful sometimes to work among so many
who thought him just a commodity but then one day
he found a skater who could waltz to the
tune he danced to.

They fell on a mattress, compounding desire with
fierce resolve, and became two eagles soaring eight
miles high, hoping getting stoned that way wasn't
going to cement their hearts into some public drinking
fountain whose inscription is the forgotten key in an
old leather briefcase left in a box in the attic until the
farm is sold and the key case
is given to the kids to play with.

Though that really didn't seem so bad after all
when they thought about it.

I have
in my own
way
threaded my
own needle, sewn
my
own oats
wild or tame
stayed
in my own
groove
(not to
say stuck I
hope)
though lately
there is a
certain
sameness to
it all, given
a
definite aging
that for the
present
seems to
continue pretty nicely
overall
considering how
much patchwork life
requires

Practice Session

Weak or busy, disturbed by some older rhythm, I repeat the same storms and silences you've all heard before

as predictable as weather or engine-room breakdowns, rods thrown, gas tank empty burning too much midnight oil

but emerge unscathed protected by the rose of your love and an inherited symbolism handed down for generations that has to do with sunrises, how they recur and recur.

If only I could show you the music involved, could play it for you on some as-yet-uninvented instrument instead of merely sitting here scribbling, rehearsing and re-rehearsing this unfinished symphony.

The Real Thing

There's always a kind of contradiction in the diction of forms, as when a flower dies performing a strip-tease, a kind of visually ironic organic joke.

We're not talking profit and loss, the puzzle is something deeper
wafting on the evening air.

We watch the petals bloom and drop, we catch the scent and follow like blind dogs trying to stick our noses further into something prior to language, sniffing eagerly, yet wary, peering suspiciously, hoping we aren't barking up the wrong tree.

The mountain hermits had it right: rain on the roof, a few simple poems, a bamboo flute, no need for metaphor or simile.

The real thing itself, nothing more, just step through the doorless door.

The Sixties
(For The Human Be-In, 01-14-1967)

In a perpetual dream traditional tavern songs become kaleidoscopic crystal glassware sparkling in a mirror as the festival begins

the parade includes our float of tropical flowers: a slightly rippling ocean dappled with shards of sunlight and a golden-sand beach encircled by a reef where fish the colors of new toys present themselves for viewing

we ride by singing, naked as navel oranges

spectators stare wearing raincoats and sweaters, earmuffs and gloves, trying not to listen to our songs, trying to avoid our touch

but some join in, dancing in the streets and that changes everything!

They Tell Me The Waves

They tell me the waves washed right through the all-night Seagull restaurant perched at the end of the pier.

The breakers licked up everything in sight then left without paying the bill. It was no prank just Mother Nature having her way.

"Here's what you get," she said, cocking one hip and looking coquettishly over her shoulder as she sashayed away, "for building where things don't belong."

To Eric Dolphy, Yes!

First in the hearts of Creole nightblooming jazzmen
blowing cool ripplefingered strings of notes over the
stones on the bed of life growing melodic orchids
secretly from horns of plenty of bliss in neonjungle
nightmare

from bubbling woodwind depths of bass clarinet
to ultimate fluted highnotes covering the sonic
spectrum bouquets of brilliant beauty to
counterbalance all the bloodings borne by others

till your own internal hemorrhage wrote the coda
no repeat sign
tombstoning the joys you bluely blew
but leaving your amazingly graceful music to rapture
succeeding soulmates in sensuous succor
ringing in a new jazz age to awestruck ears:

THAT SOUND!
THAT SOUND!

Velvet More Or Less

The days go by too fast now
to see anything more than a blur

as the zenmen say: "The doorknob turns
but no one turns it."

Meanwhile, dancing ladies go separate ways
in slippers made of velvet

and their counterparts in passes of twos
their golden mates
recline in velvet jackets

and the touch of the ladies' toes
dancing on moonlit frozen spines
when it's 32 below
is like iced velvet

so you roll over
seeking that warm place of velvet

but it's only a mutual softness that's being felt
nothing more
and nothing velvet less.

War, From A to Z

The unbearable being of lightness is a switch just beyond reach for most. What we usually grasp is only another violent revolution of The Wheel.

From Acton to Zama, the list of famous battles is as long as history. Now all are forgotten but the most recent though some re-erupt century after century.

Who fought? Where? Why? No one but scholars remembers engagements that seemed more important than spring, than wives, than even the children to whom the pattern was handed down as a sacred bequest, to be passed along no matter what.

Till We Have Faces

That morning's ice, no more than a brittle film, had cracked and was floating on an updraft of politics ... summer hot air as it were ... slowly melting like open admiration over the face of Wright Diehl, the man who a dozen times in the past had explained events as the outcome of character or intentions, the personal defeat of this or that statesman ... or the boom of water in the rising gorge. Now he sat stringing himself out endlessly into the hazy noonday sunshine ... meanwhile, nearby, Moira Mayheekana, gifted with sound, obstinate, practical common sense, swayed mischievously in the evanescent wind, sand and stars ... standing out against the edge of day while their son Form shrieked joyfully in his winding sheet. At nightfall, with the hoarse clamor of a dreamboat steamboat barking out at sea guiding myriads of tiny flames across the ocean, came an odor of parrots, cockatoos and art dealers wafting across the hours to his ears with memories of a curious sense of relief. "That fellow I knocked down was her brother," he recalled absently, presently gazing at the subject. "Mine, too." He laughed then, a golden necklace of laughter links from his throat cast out into the gracious evening breeze like blown kisses, lusty in the true style of the old court. "Till we have faces! Till we have faces!" he called, stooping to pick up a fallen sparrow at his feet, amazed to find that it was only his shoe that had come off.

About The Author

Robert Loomis is a retired San Francisco Bay Area newspaper journalist, a published poet, and the author of *SCORE Memoirs of A Weed Smuggler*, an as-told-to story of a 1960s marijuana smuggler. Some of his poems have been published in Brushfire, Dragonfly and Modern Haiku. He is also a singer/songwriter and musician who plays in three local bands, The Irish Newsboys, The UnConcord and Blue Eyed Grass. He has self-produced two albums, *Raw Cuts*, a five-song EP of his originals, and *California Dreamin'*, a CD of original songs played on Native American flutes. He is married, the father of two children and a resident of the East Bay.

Made in the USA
Columbia, SC
22 October 2021